Olive Schreiner

The South African Question

Olive Schreiner

The South African Question

ISBN/EAN: 9783337228347

Printed in Europe, USA, Canada, Australia, Japan

Cover: Foto ©ninafisch / pixelio.de

More available books at **www.hansebooks.com**

THE SOUTH AFRICAN QUESTION

BY

AN ENGLISH SOUTH AFRICAN
(*Olive Schreiner*)
AUTHOR OF "THE STORY OF AN AFRICAN FARM," "DREAMS," ETC

CHICAGO
CHARLES H. SERGEL COMPANY
1899

> *"Then let us pray that come it may,*
>   *As come it will for a' that;*
> *That truth and worth, o'er a' the earth,*
>   *May bear the gree, and a' that;*
> *For a' that, and a' that;*
>   *It's coming yet, for a' that;*
> *That man to man, the world o'er,*
>   *Shall brothers be for a' that."*

*   *   *   *   *   *   *   *

> *"Put up thy sword: they that hold the sword shall perish by the sword."*

*   *   *   *   *   *   *   *

THE SOUTH AFRICAN QUESTION.

Many views have found expression in the columns of papers during the last weeks. The working man only a few weeks or months from England has expressed his opposition to those stratagems with war for their aim which would leave him without the defence he has at present from the pressure of employers. Journalists only a few years, months, or weeks from Europe, have written, not perhaps expressing a desire for war, but implying it might be well if the wave swept across South Africa, and especially across that portion which is richest in mineral wealth, and, therefore, more to be desired.

South Africans and men from Europe alike have written deprecating war, because of the vast suffering and loss it would occasion to individuals. Dutch and English South Africans have written (as one in an able and powerful letter dated from Vrededorp, which appeared a few days ago) proving the injustice that would be inflicted on the people of Africa, the violation of treaties and trust. But, amid all this chorus of opinion there is one voice which, though heard, has not yet been heard with that distinctness and fulness which its authority demands—it is the voice of the African-born Englishman who loves England, the man who, born in South Africa, and loving it as all men, who are men, love their birthland, is yet an Englishman, bound to England not only by ties of blood, but that much more intense passion which springs from personal contact alone. Our position is unique, and it would seem that we are marked out, at the present juncture of South African affairs, for an especial function, which imposes on us, at whatever cost to ourselves, the duty of making our voices heard and taking our share in the life of our two nations, at their

MOST CRITICAL JUNCTURE.

For, let us consider what exactly our position is.

Born in South Africa, our eyes first opened on these African hills and plains; around us, of other parentage but born with us in the land, our birth-fellows, were men of another white race; and we grew up side by side with them. Is it strange that, like all men living, who have the hearts of men, we learnt to love this land in which we first saw light? In after years, when we left it, and lived months or years across the seas, is it strange we carried it with us in our hearts? When we stood on the Alps and looked down on the lakes and forests of Switzerland, that we have said, "This is fair, but South Africa to us is fairer?" That when on the top of Milan Cathedral and we have looked out across the wide plains of Lombardy, we have said, "This is noble; but nobler to us are the broad plains of Africa, with their brown kopjes shimmering in the translucent sunshine?" Is it strange that when, after long years of absence, years it may be of success and the joy which springs from human fellowship and youth, our ship has cast its anchor in sight of Table Bay, and the great front of Table Mountain has reared up before us, a cry of passionate joy has welled up within us; and when we saw the black men with their shining skins unloading in the docks, and the rugged faces of South Africans, browned with our African sun, we put our foot on the dear old earth again, and our hearts have cried: "We are South Africans! We have come back again to our land and to our people?" Is it strange that when we are in other lands and we fear that death approaches us, we say: "Take me back! We may live away from her, but when we are dead we must lie on her breast. Bury us among the kopjes where we played when we were children, and let the iron stones and red sand cover us?" Is it strange that wherever we live we all want to go home to die; and that the time comes when we know that dearer far to us than fame or success is one little handful of our own red South African earth? Is it strange that, when the

TIME OF STRESS AND DANGER

comes to our land, we realize what, perhaps, we were but dimly conscious of before, that we are Africans, that for this land and people we could live—if need be, we could die?

Is it strange we should feel this? The Scotchman feels it for his heathery hills, the Swiss for his valleys. All men who are men feel it for the land of their birth!

What is strange is not that we have this feeling, but that, side by side with it, we have another. We love Africa, but we love England also. It is not merely that when for the first time we visit the old nesting place of our people it is rich for us with associations, that we tread it for the first time with something of the awe and reverence with which men tread an old cathedral, rich with remains of the great dead and past; it is not merely that the associations of language and literature bind us to it, nor that in some city or country churchyard we stand beside the graves of our forefathers, and trace on mould-eaten stones the names we have been familiar with in Africa, and bear as our own; nor is it that we can linger yet on the steps of the church where our parents were united before they moved to the far South, and made of us South Africans. Beyond all these impersonal, and more or less intellectual ties, we form a personal one with England. Whether we have gone home as students to college or university, or for purposes of art, literature, or professional labor, as time passes there springs up around us

A NETWORK OF TENDER BONDS;

there are formed the closest friendships our hearts will ever know, such as are formed only in the spring time of life; there is gained our first deep knowledge of life, and there grow up within us passions and modes of thought we will carry with us to our graves. After years, it may be after many years, when we return, on the walls of our study in South Africa we still keep fastened in memory of the past the old oar with which we won our first boating victory on Cam or Thames; and the faces of the men who shared our victory with us still look down at us from our walls. Not dearer to any Englishman is the memory of his Alma Mater than to him who sits thousands of miles off in the South, and who, as he smokes his last pipe of African Boer or Transvaal tobacco, is visited often by memories of days that will never fade, evenings on the river with bright faces and soft voices, long midnight conclaves over glimmering fires, when, with voices and hearts as young and glowing as our own, we discussed all problems of the universe and longed to go out into life that we might settle them—they come back to us with all the glitter and light which hangs only about the remembrances of youth: and for many of us the memory of fog-smitten London is inextricably blended with the all profoundest emotions, the most passionate endeavors, noblest relations our hearts will ever know. The steamers that come weekly to South Africa are not for us merely vessels bringing news from foreign lands; nor do they merely bring for us the intellectual pabulum which feeds our mental life; they bring us

"NEWS FROM HOME."

In London houses, in country cottages, in English manufacturing towns, are men and women whose life and labor, whose joy and sorrows our hearts will follow to the end, as theirs will follow ours to the end, and across the seas our hands will always be interknit with theirs. Our labor, our homes, our material interests, may all be in South Africa, but a bond of love so strong that six thousand miles of sea can only stretch it, but never sever it, binds us to the land and the friends we loved in our youth. We are South Africans, but intellectual sympathies, habits, personal emotions, have made us strike deep roots across the sea; and when the thought flashes on us, we may not walk the old streets again or press the old hands, pain rises which those only know whose hearts are divided between two lands. We are South Africans, but we are not South Africans only—we are Englishmen also:

> Dear little Island,
> Our heart in the sea!

If to-morrow hostile fleets encompassed England, and the tread of foreign troops was on her soil, she would not need to call to us; we would stand beside her before she had spoken. This is

OUR EXACT POSITION.

Side by side with us in South Africa are other South Africans whose position is not and cannot be exactly what ours is. Shading away from us by imperceptible degrees, stand, on one side of us, those English South Africans who, racially English, yet know nothing or little personally of her; the grandparents, and not the parents of such men, have left England; they are proud of being Englishmen, proud of England's great record and great names, as a man is proud of his grandmother's family, but they are before all things essentially South African. They desire to see England increase and progress, and to remain in harmony and union with her while she does not interfere with internal affairs of South Africa, but they do not and cannot feel to her as those of us do whose love is personal and whose intellectual sympathies center largely in England.

Yet further from us on the same side stand our oldest white fellow South Africans; who were, many, not of English blood originally, though among that body of early white settlers, men who preceded us in South Africa by three centuries, were a few with English names, and though by intermarriage Dutch and English South Africans are daily and hourly blending, the bulk of these folk were Dutchmen from Holland and Friesland, with a few Swedes, Germans and Danes, and later was intermingled with them a strong strain of Huguenot blood from France. These men were mainly of that folk, which, in the sixteenth century, held Philip and the Spanish Empire at bay, and struck the first death-blow into the heart of that mighty Imperial system whose death-gasp we have witnessed to-day. A brave, free, fearless folk with the

BLOOD OF THE OLD SEA KINGS

in their veins; a branch of that old Teutonic race which came with the Angles and Saxons into England and subdued the Britons, and who, in the persons of the Franks, entered Gaul, and spread its blood across Europe. They are a people most nearly akin to the English of all European folk, in language, form and feature resembling them, and in a certain dogged persistence, and an inalienable indestructible air of personal freedom.

Even under the early Dutch Government of the East India Company, they were not always restful and resented interference and external control. They frequently felt themselves * "ondergedrukt," and, taking their guns, and getting together wife and children and all that they had, and inspanning their wagons, they † trekked away from the scant boards of civilization into the wilderness, to form homes of freedom for themselves and their descendants.

In 1795 England obtained the Cape as the result of European complications, and the South African people, without request or desire on their part, were given over to England. England retired from the Cape in 1803, but, owing to other changes in Europe, she took the Cape again in 1806, and has since then been the

---

*Ondergedrukt—oppressed.
†Trekked—moved, traveled.

GUARDIAN OF OUR SEAS,
and the strongest power in our land. Since that time, for the last ninety years, Englishmen have slowly been added to the population, but the men of Dutch descent still form the majority of white South Africans throughout the Cape Colony, Free State, and Transvaal, outnumbering at the present day, even with the accession of the foreigners (Uitlanders mean foreigners in Dutch) to the goldfields of the Transvaal, those of English descent, as probably about two to one.

So we of England became stepmother to this South African people. We English are a virile race. There is perhaps no one with a drop of English blood in his veins who does not feel pride in that knowledge. We are a brave and, for ourselves, a freedom-loving race; the best of us have nobler qualities yet—we love justice; we admire courage and the love of freedom in others as well as ourselves; and we find it difficult to put our foot on the weak, it refuses to go down. At times, whether as individuals or as a nation, we are capable of the

MOST HEROIC MORAL ACTION.

The heart swells with pride when we remember what has been done by Englishmen, at different times and in different places, in the cause of freedom and justice, when they could meet with no reward and had nothing to gain. Such an act of justice on the part of the English nation was done in 1881 when Gladstone gave back to the Transvaal the independence which had been mistakenly taken. I would not say policy had no part in the action of the wise old man. No doubt that keen eagle-eye had fixed itself closely on the truth which all history teaches that a colony of Teutonic folk cannot be kept permanently in harmony and union with the Mother Country by any bond but that of love, mutual sympathy and honor. The child may be reduced by force to obedience; but time passes and the child becomes a youth; the youth may be coerced; but the day comes when the youth becomes a man, and there can be no coercion then. If the mother wishes to retain the affection of the man, she must win it from the youth. This the wise old man saw; but I believe that, over and above the wisdom, he saw the right, and the action was no less heroic because it was wise; for other men see truth who have not the courage to follow her, and accept present loss for a gain which lies across the centuries.

We English are a fearless folk, and in the main I think we seek after justice, but we have our faults. We are not a sympathetic or a quickly comprehending people; we are slow and we are proud; we are shut in by a certain

SHELL OF HARD RESERVE.

There are probably few of us who have not some consciousness of this defect in our own persons; it may be a fault allied to our highest virtues, but it is a fault, and a serious one as regards our relations with peoples who come under our rule. We may and do generally sincerely desire justice; we may have no wish to oppress, but we do not readily understand wants and conditions distinct from our own. Here and there great Englishmen have appeared in South African history as elsewhere (such as Sir William Porter and Sir George Grey) who have been able to throw themselves sympathetically into the entire life of the people about, to love them, and so to comprehend their wants and win their affections. Such men are the burning and shining lights of our Imperial and Colonial system, but they are not common. Undoubtedly the officials sent out to rule the Cape in the old days were generally men who earnestly desired to do their duty; but they did not always understand the folk they had to rule. They were generally simple soldiers, brave, fearless and honorable as the English soldier is apt to be, but with hard military conceptions of government and discipline. Our

Dutch fellow South Africans are a strange folk. Virile, resolute, passionate with a passion hid far below the surface, they are at once the gentlest and the most determined of peoples. When you try to coerce them they are hard as steel encased in iron, but with a large and generous response to affection and sympathy which perhaps no other European folk gives. They may easily be deceived once; but never twice. Under the roughest exterior of the up-country Boer lies a nature strangely sensitive and conscious of personal dignity; a people who never forgets a kindness and does

NOT EASILY FORGET A WRONG.

Our officials did not always understand them; they made no allowances for a race of brave, free men inhabiting a country which by the might of their own right hand they had won from savages and wild beasts, and who were given over into the hands of a strange government without their consent or desire; and the peculiarities which arose from their wild free life were not always sympathetically understood; even their little language, the South African "Taal," a South African growth so dear to their hearts, and to all those of us who love indigenous and South African growths, was not sympathetically and gently dealt with. The men, well meaning, but military, tried with this fierce, gentle, sensitive, free folk force, where they should have exercised a broad and comprehensive humanity; and when they did right (as when the slaves were freed), they did it often in such manner, that it became practically wrong. A little of that tact of the higher and larger kind, which springs from a human comprehension of another's difficulties and needs, might, exercised in the old days, have saved South Africa from all white-race problems; it was not, perhaps under the conditions, could not, be exercised. The people's hearts ached under the uncompromising iron rule. In 1815 there was a rising, and it was put down. As the traveler passes by train along the railway from Port Elizabeth to Kimberley, he will come, a few miles beyond Cookhouse, to a gap between two hills; to his right flows the Fish River; to his left, binding the two hills, is a ridge of land called in South Africa a "nek." It is a spot the thoughtful Englishman passes with deep pain. In the year 1815 here were hanged five

South Africans who had taken part in the rising, and the women who had fought beside them (for the South African woman has ever stood beside the man in all his labors and struggles) were compelled to stand by and look on. The crowd of fellow South Africans who stood by them believed,

HOPED AGAINST HOPE,

to the last moment, that a reprieve would come. Lord Charles Somerset sent none, and the tragedy was completed. The place is called to-day "Schlachter's Nek," or "Butcher's Ridge." Every South African child knows the story. Technically, any government has the right to hang those who rise against its rule. Superficially it is a short way of ending a difficulty for all governments. Historically it has often been found to be the method for perpetrating them. We may submerge for a moment that which rises again more formidably for its blood bath. The mistake made by Lord Charles Somerset in 1815 was as the mistake would have been by President Kruger if, in 1896, instead of exercising the large prerogative of mercy and magnanimity, he had destroyed the handful of conspirators who attempted to destroy the State. Both would have been within their legal right, but the Transvaal would have failed to find that path which runs higher than the path of mere law and leads towards light. Fortunately for South Africa our little Republic found it.

The reign of stern military rule at the Cape had this effect, that men and women, with a sore in their proud hearts, continued to move away from a controlling power that did not understand them. Some moved across the Orange River and joined the old "Voortrekkers" that had already gone into that country which is now the Free State. England kept a certain virtual sovereignty over that territory, till, in 1854, she grew weary of the expense it cost her, and withdrew from it in spite of the representations of certain of its inhabitants who sent a deputation to England to request her to retain it. Thereupon the folk organized an independent State and Government; and the little land, peopled mainly by men of Dutch descent, but largely intermingled with English who lived with them on terms of the greatest affection and unity, has become one of the most

PROSPEROUS, WELL-GOVERNED AND PEACEFUL communities on earth. Others, much the larger part of the people, moved further; they crossed the Vaal River, and in that wild northern land, where no Englishman's foot had passed, they founded after some years the gallant little Republic we all know to-day as the Transvaal. How that Republic was founded is a story we all know. Alone, unbacked by any great Imperial or national power, with their old flint-lock guns in their hands as their only weapons, with wife and children, they passed into that yet untrodden land. The terrible story of their struggles, the death of Piet Retief and his brave followers, killed by treachery by the Zulu Chief, Dingaan, the victory of the survivors over him, which is still commemorated by their children as Dingaan's Day, the whole, perhaps, the most thrilling record of the struggle and suffering of a people in founding their State that the world can anywhere produce. Paul Kruger can still remember how, after that terrible fight, women and children left alone in the fortified laager, he himself being but a child, they carried on bushes to fortify the laager, women with children in their arms, or pregnant, laboring with strength of men to entrench themselves against evil worse than death. Here in the wilderness they planted their homes, and founded their little State. Men and women are still living who can remember how, sixty years ago, the spot where the great mining camp of Johannesburg now stands was a great silence where they drew up their wagon and planted their little home, and

FOUGHT INCH BY INCH

with wild beasts to reclaim the desert. In this great northern land, which no white man had entered or desired, they planted their people, and loving it as men only can love the land they have suffered and bled for, the gallant little Republic they raised they love to-day as the Swiss loves his mountain home and the Hollander his dykes. It is theirs, the best land on earth to them.

They had fought not for money but for homes for their wives and children; when they battled, the wives reloaded the old flint-lock guns and handed them down from the front chest of their wagon for the men who stood around defending them. It was a wild free fight, on even terms; there were no Maxim guns to mow down ebony figures by the hundred at the turn of a handle; a free even stand up fight; and there were times when it almost seemed the assagai would overcome the old flint-lock, and the voortrekkers would be swept away. The panther and the jaguar rolled together on the ground, and, if one conquered instead of the other, it was yet a fair fight, and South Africa has no reason to be ashamed of the way either her black men or her white men fought it.

If it be asked, has the Dutch South African always dealt gently and generously with the native folks with whom he came into contact, we answer, "No, he has not"—neither has any other white race of whom we have record in history. He kept slaves in the early days! Yes, and a century ago England wished to make war on her American subjects in Virginia for refusing to take the slaves she sent. There was a time when we might have vaunted some superiority in the English-African method of dealing with the native.

THAT DAY IS PAST.

The terrible events of the last five years in South Africa have left us silent. There is undoubtedly a score laid against us on this matter, Dutch and English South Africans alike; for the moment it is in abeyance; in fifty or a hundred years it will probably be presented for payment as other bills are, and the white man of Africa will have to settle it. It has been run up as heavily north of the Limpopo as south; and when our sons stand up to settle it, it will be Dutchmen and Englishmen together who have to pay for the sins of their fathers.

Such is the history of our fellow South Africans of Dutch extraction, who to-day cover South Africa from Capetown to the Limpopo. In the Cape Colony, and increasingly in the two Republics, are found enormous numbers of cultured and polished Dutch-descended South Africans, using English as their daily form of speech, and in no way distinguishable from the rest of the nineteenth century Europeans. Our most noted judges, our most eloquent lawyers, our most skillful physicians, are frequently men of this blood; the lists of the yearly examinations of our Cape University are largely filled with Dutch names, and women, as well as men, rank high in the order of merit.

It would sometimes almost seem as if the long repose the people has had from the heated life of cities, with the large tax upon the nervous system, had sent them back to the world of intellectual occupations with more than the ordinary grasp of power. In many cases they go home to Europe to study, and doubtless their college life and English friendships bind Britain close to their hearts as to ours who are English-born. The present State Attorney of the Transvaal is a man who has taken some of the highest honors Cambridge can bestow. Besides, there exist still our old simple farmers or Boers, found in the greatest perfection in the midland districts of the Colony, in the Transvaal and Free State, who constitute a large part of the virile backbone of South Africa. Clinging to their old seventeenth century faiths and manners, and speaking their African taal, they are yet tending to pass rapidly away, displaced by their own cultured modern children; but they still form a large and powerful body. Year by year the lines dividing the South Africans from their more lately arrived English-descent brothers are

PASSING AWAY.

Love, not figuratively but literally, is obliterating the line of distinction; month by month, week by week, one might say hour by hour, men and women of the two races are meeting. In the Colony there are few families which have not their Dutch or English connections by marriage; in another generation the fusion will be complete. There will be no Dutchmen then and no Englishmen in South Africa, but only the great blended South African people of the future, speaking the English tongue, and holding in reverend memory its founders of the past, whether Dutch or English. Already, but for the sorrowful mistakes of the last years, the line of demarcation would have faded out of sight; external impediments may tend to delay it, but they can never prevent this fusion; we are one people. In thirty years' time, the daughter of the man who landed yesterday in South Africa will carry at her heart the child of a de Villiers, and the son of the Cornish miner who lands this week will have given the name of her English grandmother to his daughter, whose mother was a le Roux. There will be nothing in forty years but the great blended race of Africans.

* * * * * * *

These South Africans, together with those of English descent, but who have been more than two generations in the country and have had no—or very little—personal and intimate knowledge and intercourse with England, may be taken as standing on one side of us. They are before all things South Africans. They have—both Dutch and English—in many cases a deep and sincere affection for the English language, English institutions, and a sincere affection for England herself. They are grateful to her for her watch over their seas; and were a Russian fleet to appear in Table Bay to-morrow and attempt to land troops, it would fly as quickly from Dutch as English bullets.

Neither Dutch nor English South Africans desire to see any other power installed in the place of England. Cultured Dutch and English Africans alike are fed on English literature, and England is their intellectual home. Even with our simplest Dutch-descent Africans the memories of

THE OLD BITTER DAYS

had almost faded, when the ghastly events, which are too well known to need referring to, awoke the old ache at the heart a few years ago. But even they would see quietly no other power standing in the place of England. "It is a strange thing," said a well-known Dutch South African to us twenty-one years ago, "that when I went to Europe to study I went to Holland, and loved the land and the people, but I felt a stranger; it was the same in Germany, the same in France. But when I landed in England I said, 'I am at home!'" That man was once a passionate lover of England, but he is now a heart-sore man. There have been representatives of England in South Africa who have been loved as dearly by the Dutch as by the English. When a few years ago there was a talk of Sir George Grey visiting South Africa on his way home from New Zealand to England, old grey-headed Dutchmen in the Free State expressed their resolve to take one more long train journey and go down to Capetown only once more to shake the hand of the old man who more than forty years before had been Governor of the Cape Colony. So deeply had a great Englishman, upholding the loftiest traditions of English justice and humanity, endeared himself to the hearts of South Africans. "God's Englishman"—not of the Stock Exchange and the Gatling gun, but of the great heart.

But great as is the bond between South Africans, whether Dutch or English, and England, caused by language, sentiments, interest and the noble record left by those large Englishmen who have labored among us, the South African pure and simple, whether English or Dutch, cannot feel to England just as we do. Their material interest may bind them to England as much as it binds us, but that deep passion for her honor, the consciousness that she represents a large spiritual factor in our lives, which, once gone, nothing replaces for us; that her right-doing is ours, and her wrongdoing is also ours; that in a manner her flag does not represent anything we have an interest in, or even that we love, but that in a curious way it is ourselves—this they cannot know. Therefore, while on our side we are connected with them by our affection for South Africa and our resolute desire for its good, our position remains not exactly as theirs. Our standpoint is at once broader and more impartial in dealing with South African questions, in that we are bound by two-fold sympathies.

On the other hand of us, who are at once South Africans and Englishmen, stand in South Africa another body of individuals who are not South African, in any sense or only partially, but to whom from our peculiar position we also stand closely bound.

Ever since the time when England took over the Cape, there has been slowly entering the country a thin stream of new settlers, English mainly, but largely reinforced by people of other nationalities. Eighty years ago, in 1820, a comparatively large body of Englishmen arrived at once, and are known as the British Settlers. They settled at first mainly in Albany, and certain of their descendants are to-day, in some senses, almost as truly and typically South African as the older Dutch settlers.

THEIR LOVE FOR AFRICA

is intense. Some years later a large body of Germans were brought to the Kingwilliams town division of South Africa. They, too, became farmers, and their descendants are already true

South Africans. For the rest, for years men continually dribbled in slowly and singly from other countries. Whether they came out in search of health, as clergymen, missionaries, or doctors, or in search of manual employment, or as farmers, they almost all became, or tended to become almost immediately, South Africans. They settled in the land permanently among people who were permanent inhabitants, they often married women born in South Africa, and their roots soon sank deeply into it. They brought us no new problem to South Africa. They have settled among us, living as we live, sharing our lives and interests. It is said that it takes thirty years to make a South African, and in a manner this is true. Even now, more especially in times of stress or danger, it is easy to distinguish the African-born man from the man of whatever race and however long in the country who has not been born here. But in the main these newcomers have become South Africans with quickness and to an astonishing degree, and coming in in driblets they were, so to speak, easily digested by South Africa.

But during the last few years

A NEW PHENOMENON HAS STARTED

up in South African life. The discovery of vast stores of mineral wealth in South Africa, more especially gold, has attracted suddenly to its shores a large population which is not and cannot, at least at once, be South African. This body is known under the name of the Uitlanders (literally "Foreigners").

Through a misfortune, and by no

fault of its own, the mass of this gold has been discovered mainly along the Witwatersrand, within the territory of the Transvaal Republic, and more especially at the spot where the great mining camp of Johannesburg now stands, thus throwing upon the little Republic the main pressure of the new arrivals.

To those who know the great mining camps of Klondike and Western America, it is perhaps not necessary to describe Johannesburg. Here are found that diverse and many-shaded body of humans, who appear wherever in the world gold is discovered. The Chinaman with his pigtail, the Indian Coolie, the manly Kafir, and the Half-caste; all forms of dark and colored folk are here, and outnumber considerably the white. Nor is the white population less multifarious and complex. On first walking the streets, one has a strange sense of having left South Africa, and being merely in some cosmopolitan center, which might be anywhere where all nations and colors gather round the yellow king. Russian Jews and Poles are here by thousands, seeking in South Africa the freedom from oppression that was denied that much-wronged race of men in their own birth-land; Cornish and Northumberland miners; working men from all parts of the earth; French, German and English tradesmen; while on the Stock Exchange men of every European nationality are found, though the Jew predominates. The American strangers are not large in number, but are represented by perhaps the most cultured and enlightened class in the camp, the mining engineer and large importers of mining machinery being often of that race; our lawyers and doctors are of all nationalities, while in addition to all foreigners, there is a certain admixture of English and Dutch South Africans. In the course of a day one is brought into contact with men of every species. Your household servant may be a Kafir, your washerwoman is a Half-caste, your butcher is a Hungarian, your baker English, the man who soles your boots a German, you buy your vegetables and fruit from an Indian Coolie, your coals from the Chinaman round the corner, your grocer is a Russian Jew, your dearest friend an American. This is an actual, and not an imaginary, description. Here are found the most noted prostitutes of Chicago; and that sad sisterhood created by the dislocation of our yet uncoordinated civilization, and known in Johannesburg under the name of continental women, have thronged here in hundreds from Paris and the rest of Europe. Gambling, as in all mining camps, is rife; not merely men but even women put their money into the totalisator, and

A LOW FEVER OF ANXIETY

for chance wealth feeds on us. Crimes of violence are not unknown; but, if one may speak with authority who has known only one other great mining center in its early condition, and whose information on this matter has therefore been gathered largely from books, Johannesburg compares favorably, and *very* favorably, with other large mining camps in the same stage of their existence. The life of culture and impersonal thought is largely and of necessity among a new and nomadic population absent; art and science are of necessity unrepresented; but a general alertness and keenness characterizes our population. In the bulk of our miners and working men, of our young men in banks and houses of business, we have a large mass of solid, intelligent, and invaluable social material which counter-balances that large mass of human flotsam and jetsam found in this, as in all other mining camps; while among our professional men and mining officials is found a large amount of the highest professional knowledge and efficiency. Happy would it be for the gallant little Transvaal Republic, and well for South Africa as a whole, if the bulk of this little human nature could become ours forever, if they were here to stay with us, drink out of our cup and sup out of our platter. But in most cases this is not so. The bulk of the population, and especially its most valuable and cultured elements, are here temporarily; as persons who go to Italy or the south of France for health or sunshine, who, even when they go year after year, or buy villas and settle there for a time, yet go to seek merely health and sunshine, not strike root there; and as men go to Italy for health and sunshine, the bulk of us here come to seek gold or a temporary livelihood, and for nothing more. Even our miners and working men in Johannesburg, the most stable and possibly permanent element in our population, have, in many instances, their wives and families in Cornwall or elsewhere; and when they have them here they still think of the return home for good in after years; while with the wealthier classes this is practically universal. Not only have our leading mining engineers and the great speculators not the slightest intention of staying in Johannesburg permanently; most have their wives and families in England, America, or on the Continent, and project as soon as possible a retirement from business, and return to the fashionable circles of Europe or America. Even among South African-born men the large majority of us intend returning to our own more lovely birthplaces and homes in the Colony sooner or later; and the only element which will probably form any integral part of the South African nation of the future and become subject to the Transvaal Republic is the poorer, which, from the larger advantages for labor here, will be unable to return to its natural home.

The nomadic population of Johannesburg undoubtedly consists of men who are brave and loyal citizens in their own States and nations. To-morrow,

IF AMERICA WERE IN DANGER,

probably almost every American citizen would troop back to her bosom, and spend not only life, but the wealth he had gained in South Africa from South African soil, in defending her. Every German would go home to the Fatherland; every Englishman, every Frenchman, would, as all brave men in the world's history have done, when the cry arises, "The birthland in danger!" The few Spaniards here trooped back to Spain as soon as the news of war arrived.

One of the most brilliant and able of

English journalists (a man whose opinion on any subject touching his own land we would receive almost with the reverence accruing to the man who speaks of a subject he knows well and has studied with superior abilities; but who had been only a few months in our land, and, therefore, had not full grasp of either our people or our problems, which from their complexity and many-sidedness are subjects for a life's devotion) that man, three and a half years ago, when brave little Jameson—brave, however mistaken—was sent in to capture the mines of Johannesburg for his master, and when the great mixed population of Johannesburg, Germans and French, English and Jews, Arabs and Chinamen, refused to arise and go to aid him, and when hundreds of Englishmen, Cornishmen and others fled from Johannesburg, fearing that Jameson might arrive and cause a disturbance — said that Johannesburg would be known forever in history by the name of *Judasburg!* and that the Cornish and other Englishmen who fled from the place were poltroons and cowards. But he was mistaken.

JOHANNESBURG IS NOT JUDASBURG,

and the Englishmen who fled were not poltroons. There ran in them blood as brave as any in England, and if to-morrow a hostile force attacked their birthland, those very Cornish miners and English working men would die in the last ditch defending their land. Those men were strangers here; they came to earn the bread they could with difficulty win in their own land; they were friendly treated by South Africa and made money here; but were they bound to die in a foreign land for causes which they neither knew nor cared for?

One thing only can possibly justify war and the destruction of our fellows to the enlightened and humane denizen of the nineteenth century; the unavoidable conviction that by no other means can we preserve our own life and freedom from a stronger power, or defend a weaker state or individual from a stronger. Nothing can even palliate it but so intense a conviction of a right so great to be maintained that we are willing, not merely to hire other men to fight and die for us, but to risk our own lives,

A LIFE FOR A LIFE.

This the Englishmen in Johannesburg and foreigners of all nations could not possibly feel. They were not more

bound to die to obtain control of the
gold mines of Johannesburg for a man
already wealthy or his confederates,
than to assist South Africans in defending them; or than we who visit the
south of France or Italy for health
should feel ourselves bound to remain
and die if war breaks out between the
Bonapartists and the Republicans, or
the Pope and the King. If by a process of abstract thought we have arrived at a strong conviction of a right
or human justice to be maintained by
a cause with which we have no practical concern, we may feel morally
compelled to take a part in it; but no
man can throw it in our teeth if we
refuse to die in a strange land for

A CAUSE THAT IS NOT OURS.

The Englishmen and others who refused to fight in Johannesburg, or fled rather than run the risk of remaining, pursued the only course open to wise and honorable men. Had they resolved to remain permanently in South Africa, and to become citizens of the Transvaal Republic, the case might have been otherwise. As it was, they could not run a knife into the heart of a people which had hospitably received them, and attempt to destroy a land in which they had found nothing but greater wealth and material comfort than in their own; and they could also not enter upon a deadly raid for a man whom personally the workers of Johannesburg cared nothing for, and with whom they had not a sympathy or interest in common. In leaving Johannesburg and refusing to fight, they pursued the only course left open to them by justice and honor.

Rightly to understand the problem before the little Transvaal Republic to-day, it is necessary for Englishmen to imagine not merely that, within the space of ten or twelve years, forty millions of Russians, Frenchmen and Germans should enter England, not in driblets and in time extending over half a century, so that they might, in a measure, be absorbed and digested into the original population, but instantaneously and at once; not merely, that the large bulk of them did not intend to remain in England, and were there merely to extract wealth; not merely, that the bulk of this wealth was exported at once to other countries enriching Russia, France and Germany out of the products of English soil; that would be comparatively a small matter—but, that the bulk of the wealth extracted was in the hands of a few persons, and that these persons were opposed to the continued freedom and independence of England, and were attempting by the use of the wealth they extracted from England to stir up Russia and France against her, that through the loss of her freedom they might the better obtain the command of her wealth and lands. When the Englishman has vividly drawn this future for himself, he will hold, as nearly as is possible, in a nutshell an image of the problem which the people and government of the Transvaal Republic are called on to face to-day; and we put it straightly to him whether this problem is not one of

INFINITE COMPLEXITY AND DIFFICULTY?

Much unfortunate misunderstanding has arisen from the simple use of the terms "capitalist" and "monopolist" in the discussion of South African matters. Without the appending of explanation, they convey a false impression. These terms, so familiar to the students of social phenomena in Europe and America, are generally used in connection with a larger, but a quite distinct body of problems. The terms "capitalism," "monopolist," and "millionaire" are now generally associated with the question of the forming of "trusts," "corners," etc., and the question whether it is desirable that society should so organize itself that one man may easily obtain possession of twenty millions, while the bulk of equally intelligent and equally laborious men obtain little or nothing from the labor of humanity. This question is a world-wide question; it is not one in any sense peculiarly South African; it is a world-wide problem, which, as the result of much thought, careful consideration and many experiments, the nations of the civilized world will be called to adjudicate upon during the twentieth century; but it is not the question with which South Africa stands face to face at this moment. The question before us is not: Shall one South African possess twenty millions, live in his palace, live on champagne, have his yacht in Table Bay, and deck women with a hundred thousand pounds' worth of jewels, while the South African next door has nothing? This is not our question. Our problem is not the problem of America. In America there are many individuals possessing wealth amounting to many millions, but when the United States in their entirety is taken the £40,000,000 of the richest individual sink to nothing; and, were it the desire of the richest millionaire in the States

TO CORRUPT AND PURCHASE

the whole population for political purposes, he could not pay so much as £1 a head to the 80,000,000 inhabitants of the country. Further, the bulk of American millionaires are American! They differ in no respect, except in their possession of large wealth, in interest or affections, from the shoemaker in the alley or the farmer at his plough. They are American citizens; their fate is bound up with that of the land they live in; their ambitions are American. If a great misfortune should overtake America to-morrow there is no reason to suppose that the heart of a Rockefeller or a Vanderbilt would not ache as that of the simplest cowboy in the States. When they die, it is to American institutions that they leave their munificent donations, and the colleges and public institutions of America are endowed by them. The mass even of that wealth they expend on themselves is expended in America, and, whether they will or no, returns to the people of the country in many forms. The millionaires of America are and remain Americans; and the J. Gould who should expend his millions in stirring up war between the North and South, or in urging England to attack and slay American citizens, would be dealt with by his fellow-subjects, whether millionaires or paupers, with expedition. The question whether the conditions which lead to such vast accretions of fortune in the hands of private individuals is a desirable one and of social benefit is an open one, and a fair field for impartial discussion; but, whatever decision is arrived at with regard to millionaires and private monopoly as they exist in Europe or the United States, it has little or no bearing on the problem of South Africa, which is totally distinct.

South Africa is a young country, and taken as a whole it is an arid, barren country agriculturally. Our unrivalled climate, our sublime and rugged natural scenery,

THE JOY AND PRIDE of the South African heart, is largely the result of this very aridity and rockiness. Parts are fruitful, but we have no vast corn-producing plains, which for generations may be cultivated almost without replenishing, as in Russia and America; we have few facilities for producing those vast supplies of flesh which are poured forth from Australia and New Zealand; already we import a large portion of the grain and flesh we consume. We may, with care, become a great fruit-producing country, and create some rich and heavy wines, but, on the whole, agriculturally, we are, and must remain, as compared with most other countries, a poor nation. Nor have we any great inland lakes, seas, and rivers, or arms of the sea, to enable us to become a great maritime or carrying people. One thing only we have which saves us from being the poorest country on the earth, and should make us one of the richest. We have our vast stores of mineral wealth, of gold and diamonds, and probably of other wealth yet unfound. This is all we have. Nature has given us nothing else; we are a poor people but for these. Out of the veins running through rocks and hills, and the mud-beds, heavy with jewels, that lie in our arid plains, must be reared and created our great national institutions, our colleges and museums, our art galleries and universities; by means of these our system of education must be extended; and on the material side, out of these must the great future of South Africa be built up—or not at all. The discovery of our mineral wealth came somewhat suddenly upon us. We were not prepared for its appearance by wise legislative enactments, as in New Zealand or some other countries. Before the people of South Africa as a whole had had time to wake up to the truth and to learn the first

GREAT AND TERRIBLE LESSON,

our diamonds should have taught us the gold mines of the Transvaal were discovered.

We South Africans, Dutch and English alike, are a curious folk, strong, brave, with a terrible intensity and perseverance, but we are not a sharp people well versed in the movements of the speculative world. In a few years the entire wealth of South Africa, its mines of gold and diamonds, its coal fields, and even its most intractable lands, from the lovely Hex River Valley to Magaliesberg, had largely passed into the hands of a very small knot of speculators. In hardly any instances are they South Africans. That they were not South African-born would in itself matter less than nothing, had they thrown in their lot with us, if in sympathies, hopes, and fears they were one with us. They are not. It is not merely that the wealth which should have made us one of the richest peoples in the world has left us one of the poorest, and is exported to other countries, that it builds palaces in Park Lane, buys yachts in the Mediterranean, fills the bags of the croupiers at Monte Carlo, decks foreign women with jewels, while our citizens toil in poverty; this is a small matter. But those men are not of us! That South Africa we love whose great future is dearer to us than our own interests, in the thought of whose great and noble destiny lies the source of our patriotism and highest inspiration, for whose good in a far distant future we, Dutch and English alike, would sacrifice all in the present —this future is no more to them than the future of the Galapagos Islands. We are a hunting ground to them, a field for extracting wealth, for

BUILDING UP FAME AND FORTUNE;

nothing more. This matter does not touch the Transvaal alone; from the lovely Hex River Valley, east, west, north, and south, our lands are being taken from us, and passing into the hands of men who not only care nothing for South Africa, but apply the vast wealth they have drawn from South African soil in an attempt to corrupt our public life and put their own nominees into our parliaments, to grasp the reins of power, that their wealth may yet more increase. Is it strange that from the hearts of South Africans, English and Dutch alike, there is arising an exceedingly great and bitter cry: "We have sold our birthright for a mess of pottage! The lands, the mineral wealth which should have been ours to build up the great Africa of the future has gone into strange hands! And they use the gold they gain out of us to enslave us; they strike at our hearts with a sword gilded with South African gold! While the gold and stones remained undiscovered in the bosom of our earth, it was saved up for us and for our grandchildren to build up the great future; it is going from us never to return; and when they have rifled our earth and picked the African bones bare as the vultures clear the carcass of their prey, they will leave us with the broken skeleton!"

I think there is no broad-minded and sympathetic man who can hear this cry without sympathy. The South African question is far other than the question: Shall one man possess twenty millions while his brother possesses none? It is one far deeper.

Nevertheless, there is another side to the question. Nations, like individuals, suffer, and must pay the price, yet more for their ignorance and stupidity than their wilful crimes. He who sits supine and intellectually inert, while great evils are being accomplished, sins wholly as much as he whose positive action produces them, and must pay the same price. The man at the helm, who goes to sleep cannot blame the rock when the ship is thrown upon it, though it be torn asunder. He should have known the rock was there, and steered clear of it. It is perhaps natural

A GREAT BITTERNESS

should have arisen in our hearts towards the men who have disinherited us; but is it always just? Personally, and in private life, they may be far from being inhuman or unjust; they may be rich in such qualities; at most they remain men and brothers who differ in no way from the majority of us. We made certain laws and regulations; they took advantage of them for their own success; they have but pursued the universal laws of the business world, and of the struggle of competition. It was we who did not defend ourselves, and must take the consequences. As long as any of these men merely use the wealth they extract from Africa for their own pleasures and interest, we have not much to complain of, and must bear the fruit of our folly. The speculators who rule in Mashonaland were wiser than we; they ordained that 50 per cent of all gold mining profits should go to the government, and they retained all diamonds found as a government monopoly. We were not wise enough to do so, and the nation must suffer. But poverty is not the worst thing that can overtake an individual or a nation. In that harsh school the noblest lessons and the sturdiest virtues are learnt. The greatest nations, like the greatest individuals, have often been the poorest; and with wealth comes often what is more terrible than poverty—corruption. Not all the millionaires of Europe can prevent one man of genius being born in this land to illuminate it; not all the gold of Africa can keep us from being the bravest, freest nation on earth; no man living can shut out from our eyes the glories of our African sky, or kill one throb of our exultant joy in our great African plains; nor can all earth prevent us from growing into a great, free, wise people. The faults of the past we cannot undo; but

THE FUTURE IS OURS.

But when the men, who came penniless to our shores and have acquired millions out of our substance, are not content with their gains; when they seek to dye the South African soil which has received them with the blood of its citizens—when they seek her freedom—the matter is otherwise.

This is the problem, the main weight of which has fallen on the little South African Republic. It was that little ship which received the main blow when eighty thousand souls of all nationalities leaped aboard at once; and gallantly the taut little craft, if for a moment she shivered from stem to stern, has held on her course to shore, with all souls on board.

We put it, not to the man in the street, who, for lack of time or interest, may have given no thought to such matters, but to all statesmen, of whatever nationality, who have gone deeply into the problems of social structure and the practical science of government, and to all thinkers who have devoted time and study to the elucidation of social problems and the structure of societies and nations, whether the problem placed suddenly for solution before this little State does not exceed in complexity and difficulty that which it has almost ever been a necessity that the people of any country in the past or present should deal with? When we remember how gravely is discussed the arrival of a few hundred thousand Chinamen in America, who are soon lost in the vast bulk of the population, as a handful of chaff is lost in a bag of corn; when we recall the fact that the appearance in England of a few thousand labouring Polish and Russian Jews amidst a vast population, into which they will be absorbed in less than two generations forming good and leal English subjects, has been solemnly adverted upon as

A GREAT NATIONAL CALAMITY,

and measures have been weightily discussed for forcibly excluding them, it will assuredly be clear, to all impartial and truth loving minds, that the problem which the Transvaal Republic has suddenly had to deal with is one of transcendent complexity and difficulty. We put it to all generous and just spirits, whether of statesmen or thinkers, whether the little Republic does not deserve our sympathy, the sympathy which wise minds give to all who have to deal with new and complex problems, where the past experience of humanity has not marked out a path—and whether, if we touch the subject at all, it is not necessary that it should be in that large, impartial, truth-seeking spirit, in which humanity demands we should appreach all great social difficulties and questions?

We put it further to such intelligent minds as have impartially watched the action and endeavors of the little Republic in dealing with its great problems, whether, when all the many sides and complex conditions are considered, it has not manfully and wonderfully endeavored to solve them?

It is sometimes said that when one stands looking down from the edge of this hill at the great mining camp of Johannesburg stretching beneath, with its heaps of white sand and debris mountains high, its mining chimneys belching forth smoke, with its seventy thousand Kafirs, and its eighty thousand men and women, white or colored, of all nationalities gathered here in the space of a few years, on the spot where fifteen years ago the Boer's son guided his sheep to the water and the Boer's wife sat alone at evening at the house door to watch the sunset, we are looking upon one of the most wonderful spectacles on earth. And it is wonderful; but, as we look at it, the thought always arises within us of something more wonderful yet—the marvelous manner in which a little nation of simple folk, living in peace in the land they loved, far from the rush of cities and the concourse of men, have risen to the difficulties of their condition; how they, without instruction in statecraft, or traditionary rules of policy, have risen to face their great difficulties, and have sincerely endeavored to meet them in a large spirit, and have largely succeeded. Nothing but that

CURIOUS AND WONDERFUL INSTINCT for statecraft and the organization and arrangement of new social conditions which seem inherent as a gift of the blood to all those peoples who took their rise in the little deltas on the northeast of the continent of Europe, where the English and Dutch peoples alike took their rise, could have made it possible. We do not say that the Transvaal Republic has among its guides and rulers a Solon or a Lycurgus; but it has to-day, among the men guiding its destiny, men of brave and earnest spirit, who are seeking manfully and profoundly to deal with the great problems before them in a wide spirit of humanity and justice. And, we do again repeat, that the strong sympathy of all earnest and thoughtful minds, not only in Africa, but in England, should be with them.

Let us take as an example one of the simplest elements of the question, the enfranchisement of the new arrivals. Even those of us, who with the present writer are sometimes denominated "the fanatics of the franchise," who hold that that state is healthiest and strongest, in the majority of cases, in which every adult citizen, irrespective of sex or position, possesses a vote, base our assertion on the fact that each individual forming an integral part of the community has their all at stake in that community; that the woman's stake is likely to be as large as the man's, and the poor man's as the rich; for each has only his all, his life; and that their devotion to its future good, and their concern in its health is likely to be equal; that the state gains by giving voice to all its integral parts. But the ground is cut from under our feet when a large mass of persons concerned are *not* integral portions of the State, but merely temporarily connected with it, have no interest in its remote future, and only a commercial interest in its present. We may hold (and we personally very strongly hold) that the moment a stranger lands in a country, however ignorant he may be of its laws, usages, and interests, if he intends to remain permanently in it, and incorporates all his life and interest with it, he becomes an integral part of the State, and should as soon as possible be given the power of expressing his will through its legislature; but the

PRACTICAL AND OBVIOUS DIFFICULTY

at once arises of determining who, in an uncertain stream of strangers who suddenly flow into a land, *is* so situated! I may go to Italy, accompanied by two friends; we may hire the same house between us (to use a homely illustration); there may be no external evidence of difference in our attitude; yet I may have determined to live and die in Italy; I may feel a most intense affection for its people and its institutions, and a great solicitude over its future. The first man who accompanies me may feel perfectly indifferent to land and people, and be there merely for health, leaving again as soon as it is restored. The second may be animated by an intense hatred of Italy and Italians; he not only may not wish well to the nation, but may desire to see it downtrodden by Austria, and its inhabitants destroyed. By enfranchising me the moment I arrived, the Italian nation would gain a faithful and devoted citizen, who would sacrifice all for her in time of danger, and devote thought in times of peace; in enfranchising immediately the second man, they would perform an act entirely negative and indifferent without loss or gain either way; in enfranchising the third man, they would perform an act of minor social suicide. Yet it would be impossible at once, and from any superficial study to discover our differences!

THE GREAT SISTER REPUBLIC

across the water has met these difficulties by instituting a probationary residence of two years, after which by taking a solemn oath renouncing all allegiance to any foreign sovereign or land, more especially to the ruler of

England and the English nation, and declaring their wish to live and die citizens of the United States, the new comers are, after a further residence of another three years, fully enfranchised, and become citizens of the American Republic. In this, as in many other cases, it would appear that the great Republic has struck on a wise and practical solution to a complex problem; and in this matter, as in many others, we, personally, should like to see the action of the great sister Republic followed. But thoughtful minds may suggest, on the other hand, that, while in America, at least at the present day, the newly enfranchised burgher receives but one-sixteen millionth of the State power and of governmental control on his enfranchisement, in a small state like the Transvaal each new burgher receives over eight hundred times that power in the government and control of the country, and that this makes a serious difference in the importance of making sure of the loyalty and sincerity of your citizen before you enfranchise him. We see this, and there is something to be said for it. It has been held by many sincerely desirous of arriving at a just and balanced conclusion, that, in a Republic situated as the Transvaal is, a longer residence and the votes of a certain proportion of the already enfranchised citizens are necessary before the vast rights conferred by citizenship in a small purely democratic State are granted. The terms for the enfranchisement for foreigners in England yield us no instructive analogy; for, in a country with an hereditary sovereign and an hereditary Upper House the enfranchised foreigner receives only a minute fraction of the power conferred on the elector in a pure democracy. The little Russian Jew who has a vote given him in London can never become the supreme head of the State, can never sit in or vote for members of the Upper House, and receives only the minute fractional power of voting for members of the Lower. It is

IN A PURE DEMOCRACY

where the people are the sovereign and represent in themselves the hereditary ruler, the hereditary Upper House, and the Lower House combined, that the personnel of each accredited citizen becomes all important. The greater the stability and immobility at one end of a State, the greater the mobility and instability which may be allowed at the other end, without endangering the stability of the State as a whole, or the healthy performance of its functions. Even on this comparatively small question of the franchise it is evident that the problem before the little Transvaal Republic is one of much complexity, and on which minds broadly liberal and sincerely desirous of attaining to the wisest and most humane and most enlightened judgment may sincerely differ.

Of those other and far more serious problems which the Republic faces in common with South Africa, there is no necessity here to speak further; the thoughtful mind may follow them out for itself. Time and experiment must be allowed for the balance of things to adjust themselves.

South Africa has need of more citizens leal and true. Whoever enters South Africa and desires to become one of us, to drink from our cup and sup from our platter, to mix his seed with ours and build up the South Africa of the future—him let us receive with open arms. From great mixtures of races spring great peoples. The scorned and oppressed Russian Jew, landing here to-day, vivified by our fresh South African breezes, may yet be the progenitor of the Spinoza and Maimonides of the great future South Africa, who shall lead the world in philosophy and thought. The pale German cobbler who with his wife and children lands to-day, so he stays with us and becomes one with us, may yet be the father of the greater Hans Sachs of Africa; and the half-starved Irish peasant become the forerunner of our future Burkes and William Porters. The rough Cornish miner, who is looking out with surprised eyes at our new South African world to-day, may yet give to us our greatest statesmen and noblest leader. The great African nation of the future will have its foundations laid on stones from many lands. Even to the Coolie and the Chinaman, so he comes among us, we personally should say: Stretch forth the hand of brotherhood. We may not desire him, we may not intentionally bring him among us, but, so he comes to remain with us, let South Africa be home to him.

"Be not unmindful to entertain strangers, for some have thereby entertained angels unawares."

* * * * *

We, English South Africans of to-day, who are truly South African, loving

THE LAND OF OUR BIRTH,

and men inhabiting it, yet bound by intense and loving ties, not only of intellectual affinity but of personal passion, to the homeland from which our parents came, and where the richest formative years of our life were passed, we stand to-day midway between these two great sections of South African folk, the old who have been here long and the new who have only come; between the home-land of our fathers and the love-land of our birth; and it would seem as though, through no advantage of wisdom or intellectual knowledge on our part, but simply as the result of the accident of our position and of our double affections, we are fitted to fulfil a certain function at the present day, to stand, as it were, as mediators and interpreters between those our position compels us to sympathize with and so understand, as they may not, perhaps, be able to understand each other.

Especially at the present moment has arrived a time when it is essential that, however small we may feel is our inherent fitness for the task, we should not shrink nor remain silent and inactive, but exert by word and action that peculiar function which our position invests us with.

* * *

If it be asked, why at this especial moment we feel it incumbent on us not to maintain silence, and what that is which compels our action and speech, the answer may be given in one word—WAR!

The air of South Africa is

HEAVY WITH RUMORS;

inconceivable, improbable, we refuse to believe them; yet, again and again they return.

There are some things the mind refuses seriously to entertain, as the man who has long loved and revered his mother would refuse to accept the assertion of the first passer-by that there was any possibility of her raising up her hand to strike his wife or destroy his child. But much repetition may at last awaken doubt; and the man may begin to look out anxiously for further evidence.

* * *

We English South Africans are stunned; we are amazed; we say there can be no truth in it. Yet we begin to ask ourselves: "What means this unwonted tread of armed and hired soldiers on South African soil? Why are they here?" And the only answer that comes back to us, however remote and seemingly impossible is—WAR!

To-night we laugh at it, and to-morrow when we rise up it stands before us again, the ghastly doubt—war!—war, and in South Africa! War—between white men and white! *War!*—Why?—Whence is the cause?—For whom?—For what?—And the question gains no answer.

We fall to considering, who gains by war?

Has our race in Africa and our race in England interests so diverse that any calamity so cataclysmic can fall upon us, as war? Is any position possible, that could make necessary that mother and daughter must rise up in one horrible embrace, and rend, if it be possible, each other's vitals? . . Believing it impossible, we fall to considering, who is it gains by war?

There is peace to-day in the land; the two great white races, day by day, hour by hour, are blending their blood, and both are mixing with the stranger. No day passes but from the veins of some Dutch South African woman the English South African man's child is being fed; not a week passes but the birth cry of the English South African woman's child gives voice to the Dutchman's offspring; not an hour passes but on farm, and in town and village, Dutch hearts are winding about English

AND ENGLISH ABOUT DUTCH.

If the Angel of Death should spread his wings across the land and strike dead in one night every man and woman and child of either the Dutch or the English blood, leaving the other alive, the land would be a land of mourning. There would be not one household nor the heart of an African born man or woman that would not be weary with grief. We should weep the friends of our childhood, the companions of our early life, our grandchildren, our kindred, the souls who have loved us and whom we have loved. In destroying the one race he would have isolated the other. Time, the great healer of all differences, is blending us into a great mutual people, and love is moving faster than time. It is no growing hatred between Dutch and English South African born men and women that calls for war. On the lips of our babes we salute both races daily.

Then we look round through the political world, and we ask ourselves: What great and terrible and sudden crime has been committed, what reckless slaughter and torture of the innocents, that blood can alone wash out blood?

And we find none.

And still we look, asking what great and terrible difference has suddenly arisen, so mighty that the human intellect cannot solve it by means of peace, that the highest and noblest diplomacy falls powerless before it, and the wisdom and justice of humanity cannot reach it, save by the mother's drawing a sword and planting it in the heart of the daughter?

We can find none.

And again, we ask ourselves

WHO GAINS BY WAR?

What is it for? Who is there that desires it? Do men shed streams of human blood as children cut off poppy-heads to see the white juice flow?

WHO GAINS BY WAR?

Not England! She has a great young nation's heart to lose. She has a cable of fellowship which stretches across the seas to rupture. She has treaties to violate. She has the great traditions of her past to part with. Whoever plays to win, she loses.

WHO GAINS BY WAR?

Not Africa! The great young nation, quickening to-day to its first consciousness of life, to be torn and rent, and bear upon its limb, into its fully ripened manhood, the marks of the wounds—wounds from a mother's hands!

WHO GAINS BY WAR?

Not the great woman whose eighty years to-night completes,* who would carry with her to her grave the remembrance of the longest reign and the purest; who would have that when the nations gather round her bier, the whisper should go round, "That was a mother's hand; it struck no child."

WHO GAINS BY WAR?

Not the brave English soldier; there are no laurels for them here. The dying lad with hands fresh from the plough; the old man tottering to the grave, who seizes up the gun to die with it; the simple farmer who as he falls hears yet his wife's last whisper, "For freedom and our land!" and dies hearing it—these men can bind no laurels on

---
*Written on 24th May, 1899.

a soldier's brow! They may be shot, not conquered—fame rests with them. Go, gallant soldiers and defend the shores of that small island that we love; there are no laurels for you here!

WHO GAINS BY WAR?

Not we the Africans, whose hearts are knit to England. We love all. Each hired soldier's bullet that strikes down a South African, does more; it finds a billet here in our hearts. It takes one African's life—in another it kills that which will never live again.

WHO GAINS BY WAR?

There are some who *think* they gain! In the background we catch sight of misty figures; we know the old tread; we hear the rustle of paper, passing from hand to hand, and we know the fall of gold; it is an old familiar sound in Africa; we know it now! There are some who *think* they gain! Will they gain?

*   *   *   *   *

But it may be said, "What matter who goads England on, or in whose cause she undertakes war against Africans; this at least is certain, she can win. We have the ships, we have the men, we have the money."

We answer, "Yes, might generally conquers—for a time at least." The greatest empire upon earth, on which the sun never sets, with its five hundred million subjects, may rise up in its full majesty of power and glory, and crush thirty thousand farmers. It may not be a victory, but at least it will be a slaughter. We ought to win. We have the ships, we have the men, and we have the money. May there not be something else we need? The Swiss had it when they fought with Austria; the three hundred had it at Thermopylae, although not a man was saved; it goes to make a victory. Is it worth fighting if we have not got it?

I suppose there is no man who to-day loves his country who has not perceived that in the life of the nation, as in the life of the individual, the hour of external success may be the hour of irrevocable failure, and that the hour of death, whether to nations or individuals, is often the hour of immortality. When William the Silent, with his little band of Dutchmen, rose up to face the whole Empire of Spain, I think there is no man who does not recognize that the hour of their greatest victory was not when they had conquered Spain, and hurled backward the greatest Empire of the world to meet its slow imperial death; it was the hour when that little band stood alone with the waters over their homes,

FACING DEATH AND DESPAIR,

and stood, facing it. It is that hour that has made Holland immortal, and her history the property of all human hearts.

It may be said, "But what has England to fear in a campaign with a country like Africa? Can she not send out a hundred thousand or a hundred and fifty thousand men and walk over the land? She can sweep it by mere numbers." We answer yes—she might do it. Might generally conquers; not always. (I have seen a little *muur kat* attacked by a mastiff, the first joint of whose leg it did not reach. I have seen it taken in the dog's mouth, so that hardly any part of it was visible, and thought the creature was dead. But it fastened its tiny teeth inside the dog's throat, and the mastiff dropped it, and, mauled and wounded and covered with gore and saliva, I saw it creep back into its hole in the red African earth.) But might generally conquers, and there is no doubt that England might send out sixty or a hundred thousand hired soldiers to South Africa, and they could bombard our towns and destroy our villages; they could shoot down men in the prime of life, and old men and boys, till there was hardly a kopje in the country without its stain of blood, and the Karoo bushes grew up greener on the spot where men from the midlands, who had come to help their fellows, fell, never to go home. I suppose it would be quite possible for the soldiers to shoot all male South Africans who appeared in arms against them. It might not be easy, a great many might fall, but a great Empire could always import more to take their places; *we* could not import more, because it would be our husbands and sons and fathers who were falling, and when they were done we could not produce more. Then the war would be over. There would not be a house in Africa—where African-born men and women lived—without its mourners, from Sea Point to the Limpopo; but South Africa would be pacified—as Cromwell pacified Ireland three centuries ago, and she has been being pacified ever since! As Virginia was pacified in 1677; its handful of men and women in defence of their freedom were soon silenced by hired soldiers. "I care that for the power of England," said "a notorious and wicked rebel" called Sarah Drummond, as she took a small stick and broke it and lay it on the ground. A few months later her husband and all the men with him were made prisoners, and the war was over. "I am glad to see you," said Berkely, the English Governor, "I have long wished to meet you; you will be hanged in half an hour!" and he was hanged and twenty-one others with him, and Virginia was pacified. But a few generations later in that State of Virginia was born George Washington, and on the 19th of April, 1775, was fought the battle of Lexington—"Where once the embattled farmers stood, and fired a shot, heard round the world,"—and the greatest crime and the greatest folly of England's career was completed. England acknowledges it now. A hundred or a hundred and fifty thousand imported soldiers might walk over South Africa; it would not be an easy walk; but it could be done. Then from east and west and north and south would come men of pure English blood to stand beside the boys they had played with at school and the friends they had loved; and a great despairing cry would rise from the heart of Africa. But we are still few. When the war was over the imported soldiers might leave the land—not all; some must be left to keep the remaining people down. There would be quiet in the land. South Africa would rise up silently, and count her dead, and bury them. She would know the places where she found them.

South Africa would be peaceful. There would be silence, the silence of a long exhaustion—but not peace! Have the dead no voices? In a thousand farm houses black robed women would hold memory of the count, and outside under African stones would lie the African men to whom South African women gave birth under our blue sky. There would be silence, but no peace.

You say that all the fighting men in arms might have been shot. Yes, but what of the women? If there were left but five thousand pregnant South African-born women, and all the rest of their people destroyed, those women would breed up again a race like to the first.

OH, LION-HEART OF THE NORTH,

do you not recognize your own lineage

in these whelps of the South? We cannot live if we are not free!

The grandchildren and great-grandchildren of the men who lay under the stones (who will not be English then nor Dutch, but only Africans), will say, as they pass those heaps: "There lie our fathers, or great-grandfathers who died in the first great War of Independence," and the descendants of the men who lay there will be the aristocracy of Africa. Men will count back to them and say: My father or my great-grandfather lay in one of those graves. We shall know no more of Dutch or English then, we shall know only one great African people. And *we?* We, the South Africans of to-day, who are still English, who have been proud to do the smallest good so it might bring honor to England, who have vowed our vows on the honor of Englishmen, and by the faith of Englishmen—what of *us?*

What of us? We, too, have had our vision of Empire. We have seen as in a dream the Empire of England as a great banyan tree; silently with the falling of the dew and the dropping of the rain it has extended itself; its branches have drooped down and rooted themselves in the earth; in it all the fowl of Heaven have taken refuge, and under its shade all the beasts of the field have lain down to rest. Can we change it for an upas tree, whose leaves distill poison and which spells death to those who have lain down in peace under its shadow?

You have no right to take our dream from us; you have no right to kill our faith! Of all the sins England will sin if she makes war on South Africa, the greatest will be towards us.

Of what importance is the honor and faith we have given her? You say, we are but few! Yes, we are few; but all the gold of Witwatersrand would not buy one throb of that love and devotion we have given her.

Do not think that when imported soldiers walk across South African plains to take the lives of South African men and women, that it is only African sand and African bushes that are cracking beneath their tread: at each step they are breaking the fibres, invisible as air, but strong as steel, which bind the hearts of South Africans to England. Once broken they can never be made whole again; they are living things; broken, they will be dead. Each bullet which a soldier sends to the heart of a

South African to take his life, wakes up another who did not know he was an African. You will not kill us with your Lee-Metfords: you will make us. There are men who do not know they love a Dutchman; but the first three hundred that fall, they will know it.

Do not say, "But you are English, you have nothing to fear: we have no war with you!"

There are hundreds of us, men and women, who have loved England; we would have given our lives for her; but, rather than strike down one South African man fighting for freedom, we would take this right hand and hold it in the fire, till nothing was left of it but a charred and blackened bone.

I know of no more graphic image in the history of the world than

THE FIGURE OF FRANKLIN when he stood before the Lords of Council in England, giving evidence, striving, fighting, to save America for England. Browbeaten, flouted, jeered at by the courtiers, his words hurled back at him as lies, he stood there fighting for England. England recognizes now that it was he who tried to save an Empire for her; and that the men who flouted and browbeat him, lost it. There is nothing more pathetic than the way in which Americans who loved England, Washington and Franklin, strove to keep the maiden vessel moored close to the mother's side, bound by the bonds of love and sympathy, that alone could bind them. Their hands were beaten down, bruised and bleeding, wounded by the very men they came to save, till they let go the mother ship and drifted away on their own great imperial course across the seas of time.

England knows now what those men strove to do for her, and the names of Washington and Franklin will ever stand high in honor where the English tongue is spoken. The names of Hutchinson, and North, and Grafton are not forgotten also; it might be well for them if they were!

Do not say to us: "You are Englishmen; when the war is over, you can wrap the mantle of our imperial glory round you and walk about boasting that the victory is yours."

We could never wrap that mantle round us again. We have worn it with pride. We could never wear it then. There would be blood upon it, and the blood would be our brothers'.

We put it to the men of England.

In that day where should we be found; we who have to maintain English honor in the South? Judge for us, and by your judgment we will abide. Remember, we are Englishmen!

* * * * *

Looking around to-day along the somewhat over-clouded horizon of South African life, one figure strikes the eye, new to the circle of our existence here; and we eye it with something of that hope and sympathy with which a man is bound to view the new and unknown, which may be of vast possible good and beauty.

What have we in this man, who represents English honor and English wisdom in South Africa? To a certain extent we know.

We have a man honorable in the relations of personal life, loyal to friend, and above all charm of gold; wise with the knowledge of books and men; a man who could not violate a promise or strike in the dark. This we know we have, and it is much to know this; but what have we more?

The man of whom South Africa has need to-day to sustain England's honor and her Empire of the future, is a man who must possess more than the knowledge and wisdom of the intellect.

When a woman rules a household with none but the children of her own body in it, her task is easy; let her obey nature and she will not fail. But the woman who finds herself in a large strange household, where children and step-children are blended, and where all have passed the stage of childhood and have entered on that stage of adolescence where coercion can no more avail, but where sympathy and comprehension are the more needed, that woman has need of large and rare qualities springing more from the heart than from the head. She who can win the love of her strange household in its adolescence will keep its loyalty and sympathy when adult years are reached and will be rich indeed.

There have been Englishmen in Africa who had those qualities. Will

THIS NEW ENGLISHMAN OF OURS

evince them and save an Empire for England and heal South Africa's wounds? Are we asking too much when we turn our eyes with hope to him?

Further off also, across the sea we look with hope. The last of the race of great statesmen was not put into the ground with the old man of Hawarden; the great breed of Chatham and Burke is not extinct; the hour must surely bring forth the man.

We look further yet with confidence, from the individual to the great heart of England, the people. The great fierce freedom-loving heart of England is not dead yet. Under a thin veneer of gold we still hear it beat. Behind the shrivelled and puny English Hyde who cries only "gold," rises the great English Jekyll, who cries louder yet "Justice and honor." We appeal to him; history shall not repeat itself.

Nearer home, we turn to one whom all South Africans are proud of, and we would say to Paul Kruger, "Great old man, first but not last of South Africa's great line of rulers, you have shown us you could fight for freedom;

show us you can win peace. On the foot of that great statue which in the future the men and women of South Africa will raise to you let this stand written: 'This man loved freedom, and fought for it; but his heart was large; he could forget injuries and deal generously.'"

And to our fellow Dutch South Africans, whom we have learnt to love so much during the time of stress and danger, we would say: "Brothers, you have shown the world that you know how to fight; show it you know how to govern; forget the past; in that Great Book which you have taken for your guide in life, turn to Leviticus, and read there in the 19th chapter, 34th verse: 'But the stranger that dwelleth with you shall be unto you as one born among you, and thou shalt love him as thyself; for ye were strangers in the land of Egypt. I am the Lord your God.'"

Be strong, be fearless, be patient.

We would say to you in the words of the wise dead President of the Free State which have become the symbol of South Africa, *"Wacht een beetje, alles zal recht kom."* (Wait a little, all will come right.)

On our great African flag let us emblazon these words, never to take them down, "FREEDOM, JUSTICE, LOVE"; great are the two first, but without the last they are not complete.

Olive Schreiner,
2 Primrose Terrace,
Berea Estate,
Johannesburg,

June, 1899.   South African Republic.

HISTORY OF BOHEMIA,

by Robert H. Vickers,

8vo, Cloth with map and illustrations, $3.50

Endorsed by the Bohemians of America, through their national organzation, as the most complete, accurate, and sympafhetic narrative of their country's history in English.

In the compilation of his stiring narative Mr. Vickers has availed himself largely of material derived from native scources, and he deserves the thanks of English-reading students for having compressed so much substance into a single book.—*The Nation.*

Mr. Vickers has rendered a great service to Bohemia in this work, and has evidently spared no pains to make it valuable.—*Boston Herald.*

As a contribution to general historical literature, Mr. Vickers' volume is an important event. —*Chicago Evening Post.*

Robert H. Vickers has rendered a lasting service to the Bohemian residents in America * * * The body of the work bears every evidence of being a thorough and valuable contribution to Bohemian history. It is a work which fills a field hitherto altogether unoccupied. —*Chicago Evening Journal.*

CHARLES H. SERGEL COMPANY,

PUBLISHERS,   CHICAGO.

HISTORY OF PERU,

by Clements R. Markham,

C. B., F. R. S., F. S. A., President Hakluyt Society, President Royal Geographical Society, and author of "Cuzco and Lima," "Peru and India," etc.

8 vo, cloth, with maps and illustrations, $ 2.50.

The highest authority on Peruvian history.—*The Critic.*

Mr. Markham has done his work well, and with ardent love for his subject. The country is a favorite one with him, and has furnished him with matter for three monographs before the present history. In a necessarily limited space he has given the leading facts, and taken a comprehensive view from the earliest time, down almost to the current year. Not the least interesting portions are the brief but strongly individual sketches of some of the remarkable men who have figured in the annals of Peru. In a few virile paragraphs he presents the more famous generals, viceroys, presidents and patriots, The book is well equipped with maps, abounds with pictures, and has an appendix rich in its statistics and important documents. —*The Literary World.*

Mr. Markham is thoroughly at home with his subject. He possesses a strong, graphic style eminently suited to it, and the amount of information that he has managed to crowd into the space at his disposal is simply marvelous.—*New Orleans Picayune.*

CHARLES H. SERGEL COMPANY,

PUBLISHERS, CHICAGO.

HISTORY OF CHILE,

by Anson Uriel Hancock,

Author of "Old Abraham Jackson," "Coitian, A Tale of the Inca World," etc.

8vo, Cloth, with map and illustrations, $2.50

It has been Mr. Hancock's endeavour to give a "complete short history and picture of Chile in a single volume." We may congratulate him on having achieved his design. Mr. Hancock's virtures are those of painstaking chronicler. And he has those virtues in full quantity. Not that the author is without dramatic power. The concluding chapters of this valuable book on the ethnology, geology, agriculture, communications, and resources of Chile are of great interest.—*London Saturday Review*.

Within the compass of less than 500 octavo pages the author gives a succinct and rapid narrative of the history of Chile, its institutionss, the character of its people, and its present conditions, resources and outlook. He has made a painstaking examination of authorities, and has preserved a due sense of proportion.—*Boston Journal*.

It is on the period between the years 1830 and 1880, however, that the interest of the reader will concentrate itself, and recognizing this fact Mr. Hancock has spared no pains in rendering this part of the work the most brilliant and authentic. It is in every respect a thoroughly readable and accurate work, dealing with the history of a country which promises to be of much greater importance among the nations of the earth.—*Philadelphia Item*.

CHARLES H. SERGEL COMPANY,

PUBLISHERS, CHICAGO.

www.ingramcontent.com/pod-product-compliance
Lightning Source LLC
Chambersburg PA
CBHW020121170426
43199CB00009B/581